Special Needs and the National Curriculum

1991–92

The implementation of
the curricular requirements
of the Education Reform Act

A report from the Office
of Her Majesty's
Chief Inspector of Schools

London: HMSO

Office for Standards in Education
Elizabeth House
York Road
London SE1 7PH
Tel. 071-925 6800

ISBN 0 11 350013 0

CONTENTS

INTRODUCTION

Nationally, about 20 per cent of the school population have special educational needs (SEN) at some time in their schooling. This figure includes almost 2 per cent of the school population who are the subjects of statements under the Education Act 1981, over a third of whom are in ordinary schools. Since 1 August 1990 all pupils with SEN have been subject to the statutory requirements of the National Curriculum Subject Orders as they are implemented, unless they have statements which disapply or modify their National Curriculum requirements or where special directions are made under Section 19 of the Education Reform Act 1988.

This report is concerned with the response of maintained ordinary and special schools to the mandatory National Curriculum requirements over the school year from September 1991 to July 1992. It is based upon visits by HM Inspectors (HMI) to inspect work with pupils with SEN in 173 special schools, 38 ordinary primary schools, and 50 ordinary secondary schools. Altogether, just over a thousand lessons were seen. The special schools' cohort contained 109 schools with both primary and secondary age pupils, 19 schools with only primary age pupils and 45 with only secondary age range pupils.

In a total of 701 lessons inspected in special schools, 92 were at Key Stage 1, 229 at Key Stage 2 and 380 at Key Stage 3. Although these figures include lessons in all the subjects where National Curriculum Statutory orders have been implemented, 66 per cent of these lessons were in the National Curriculum core subjects of mathematics, English and science. Of the 181 lessons seen in primary schools, 78 were at Key Stage 1 and 103 at Key Stage 2; 85 per cent of these lessons were in mathematics, English or science. In secondary schools, 177 Key Stage 3 lessons were inspected, 62 per cent of them in National Curriculum core subjects.

The high percentages of lessons seen in the core subjects reflect the emphasis of the inspections and not the curricular balance in the schools themselves.

This report is based upon a sample which is not necessarily representative across ordinary and special schools. The main findings, however, broadly concur with those in the 1989-90 and 1990-91 published HMI reports *Special Needs and the National Curriculum* and are likely to provide a fair reflection of national trends as far as special schools are concerned.

MAIN FINDINGS

- Teachers in ordinary and special schools were strongly committed to the provision of full access to the National Curriculum for all pupils. However, while no Statements of Special Educational Need specified modification to or disapplication from the National Curriculum, almost half the pupils in special schools were still not receiving a satisfactorily broad and balanced curriculum which complied with National Curriculum requirements.

- Across all the schools, 28 per cent of the lessons seen were judged to be good or very good. These lessons were characterised by systematic planning based upon the National Curriculum Attainment Targets and Programmes of Study. Standards were higher for the younger than for the older pupils and there was a noticeable deterioration in the work of the pupils over the school year.

- Teachers in most schools were recording the work covered by pupils by referring to Attainment Targets, but few were using the Statements of Attainment effectively to assess each pupil's progress.

- In general the numbers of teachers were at least up to satisfactory levels and in some special schools they were above the levels recommended in the DES Circular 11/90. However, in just over half the special schools there were shortages in National Curriculum subject expertise, particularly in science, modern foreign languages (MFL) and music.

- Teachers in all types of school were highly committed to in-service education and training on the National Curriculum.

- There was a shortage of special support assistants (SSAs) in some primary schools and in over half the special schools visited.

- A persistently reported weakness of in-service training was its failure to address adequately the question of how best to match work to pupils' differing abilities, particularly in classes where the range of ability was wide.

- In more than a third of primary schools and just over half the special schools unsuitable accommodation was often an obstacle to effective teaching and learning. There were shortages of suitable books and practical materials in all types of school, lessened in some primary and special schools by voluntary funding.

THE REPORT

TEACHING AND LEARNING

Key Stage 1: Special Schools

1. In the special schools, 92 lessons were seen in Key Stage 1. The work was judged to be good or very good in 37 per cent, satisfactory in 36 per cent and less than satisfactory in 27 per cent of the lessons. Across the National Curriculum range of subjects as a whole, the percentage of lessons graded good or very good became lower as the school year progressed. This deterioration in the work of SEN pupils over the school year was a feature of all key stages, both in special and in ordinary schools. Another feature common across schools was related to the age of the pupils; standards of work and the quality of teaching were generally highest at Key Stage 1 and lowest at Key Stage 3.

2. At Key Stage 1 in special schools, good standards were more often achieved where the work was planned thoroughly, related to the National Curriculum Statements of Attainment and Programmes of Study, and set clear objectives for the pupils. In the less effective lessons the pupils often lacked the opportunity to discuss their work, for example in topics covering more than one subject, and planning was not based on the effective assessment and recording of their earlier progress.

3. In most of the work seen in Year 1 and Year 2, the pupils were working within Level 1 for the core subjects. Mathematics focused on number and shape using equipment for matching and sorting activities to establish one-to-one correspondence and shape recognition. Particularly good work was seen in English. Some good work on speaking and listening skills involved close collaboration between teachers and speech therapists. The teaching of reading was given a priority in all schools. In the early stages the pupils were generally required to listen to stories and rhymes, to recognise words and learn the phonic skills of associating sounds with symbols. The best

standards achieved in writing were often simple records of the results of investigative work in science, themes about "myself" or "my school", or a visit made to a local place of interest. Good work in science required the pupils to investigate the properties of a range of materials using touch, taste, sight and smell.

4. In lessons where teaching and learning were less than satisfactory, much of the work was pitched either at too low or, more rarely, at too high a level, and was not related to National Curriculum Programmes of Study. Poor classroom organisation or a limited range of teaching methods also related strongly to low standards of work. In mathematics, poor standards were associated with an insufficient use of practical materials and apparatus.

Key Stage 2: Special Schools

5. Of the 229 lessons seen at Key Stage 2, 29 per cent were judged to be good or very good, 34 per cent satisfactory and 37 per cent less than satisfactory. Two-thirds of the lessons in the core subjects were satisfactory or better, with some good work seen in all three areas, particularly in science. The general features associated with work of a satisfactory or better standard were as outlined for Key Stage 1.

6. The majority of the pupils in Key Stage 2 were working at National Curriculum Levels (1-3) normally assigned to Key Stage 1. In mathematics the work continued to focus mainly on number with some work on measurement. Some good use of information technology (IT) to support the work of individual pupils was seen. In speaking and listening some pupils achieved levels appropriate for Key Stage 2. This occurred when they understood the purposes of the tasks set and when the work was based upon experience such as visits or practical tasks where teachers encouraged discussion and questioning. Where the best standards of writing were achieved, the pupils drafted and re-drafted personal writing to produce work which was well within Key Stage 2 Levels. There were examples of effective use

of word-processing to support this work. Science was often organised within a theme or topic, which also included technology Attainment Targets and frequently required pupils to use equipment and make careful observations.

7. Teaching and learning of a less than satisfactory standard at Key Stage 2 in mathematics often resulted from a failure to achieve a good match of work to the spread of ability in the class. In English, poor teaching and learning were associated with the excessive use of undifferentiated worksheets and cards with whole class groups. The limited range of English Attainment Targets addressed by such materials did not contribute to improving pupils' performance. Where science standards were poor, teachers often demonstrated experiments without giving pupils opportunities to handle the equipment themselves. Another feature of poor science work was the failure of the teacher to use questions to ensure that pupils of different abilities understood the information provided and knew what to do. These limitations frequently reflected the teachers' insecurity in teaching a subject where their own knowledge was limited and where they had little professional support.

Key Stage 3: Special Schools

8. At Key Stage 3, from a total of 380 lessons observed, 22 per cent were judged to be very good or good, 35 per cent satisfactory, and 43 per cent less than satisfactory. This was little different from the findings in the previous year. Sixty-three per cent of work in the core subjects was satisfactory or better and, as at Key Stage 2, good work was seen in science.

9. A substantial proportion of pupils were still working at Levels assigned to Key Stage 1 of the National Curriculum. Teaching and learning in mathematics were mainly on number, measurement and shape, with some work on handling data. In 65 per cent of English lessons, standards of teaching and learning were satisfactory or better. English work covered the full range of English Attainment Targets, though most pupils were still

only achieving Attainment Target Levels at Key Stage 1. In 64 per cent of science lessons the standards of teaching and learning were satisfactory or better but, as in other subjects, the pupils seldom reached the Levels within the standard range for Key Stage 3.

10. Particularly poor teaching and learning in lessons with Years 7, 8 and 9 pupils were observed in schools where there had not been a satisfactory audit of the curriculum, and where the work was not related to National Curriculum Programmes of Study. In the foundation subjects, lessons in some schools were unsatisfactory because of a lack of specialist knowledge in particular subjects by teachers.

Key Stages 1 and 2: Primary Schools

11. Of the 78 lessons inspected at Key Stage 1, 47 per cent were very good or good, 28 per cent were satisfactory and 24 per cent less than satisfactory. At Key Stage 2, of the 103 lessons inspected, 31 per cent were very good or good, 39 per cent satisfactory and 30 per cent were less than satisfactory.

12. At Key Stage 1 and Key Stage 2, the satisfactory or better lessons reflected the influence of a curriculum audit which related the work to National Curriculum Programmes of Study. The tasks set were appropriately matched to the pupils' needs and clear instruction and questions on the part of the teachers enabled pupils to understand and discuss the requirements and outcomes of the tasks. In Year 1 and Year 2 the majority of the pupils with SEN were working at Level one in the core subjects. In Year 3, Year 4, Year 5 and Year 6 a significant proportion of pupils were working within the standard range assigned to Key Stage 1 (levels 1-3). Most of the mathematics in Key Stage 2 lessons focused upon number work, with less atttention given to measurement, shape and data handling. Most of the English at Key Stage 2 was directed towards Levels one and two in Attainment Target 2 and Levels one and two in Attainment

Target 3. Where additional support was provided for pupils with SEN by a teacher or SSA, the adults concerned planned and recorded the work jointly.

13. Throughout Key Stage 1 and Key Stage 2 less than satisfactory standards of teaching and learning were seen in lessons where the work was not related to National Curriculum Programmes of Study, planning did not provide the necessary match of work to ability, classroom management was generally poor, and teaching methods did not include strategies for supporting pupils with SEN.

Key Stage 3: Secondary Schools

14. Of the 177 lessons observed at Key Stage 3, 25 per cent were very good or good, 31 per cent satisfactory and 44 per cent less than satisfactory. Mathematics fared relatively well, with three-quarters of the lessons rated as satisfactory or better.

15. In Years 7, 8 and 9 the majority of pupils with SEN were not reaching Attainment Target Levels within the standard range for Key Stage 3. The work in mathematics consisted mainly of activities on number, shape and measurement Attainment Targets. Practical work was a strong feature in science and most of the pupils were able to handle apparatus well.

16. Less than satisfactory standards of teaching and learning were often associated with poorly-planned lessons in which tasks were not appropriately matched to the needs of individual pupils. Just over a quarter of the lessons seen were supported either by an additional teacher or an SSA, mainly in English and mathematics. Effective support in science, humanities and technology lessons was reduced by a lack of co-operative planning and clearly-defined roles for the adults within the classroom. Examples of lessons in MFL and IT were seen where support was needed but not available. In a small number of lessons

individual support was completely wasted as the pupil targeted for it was absent or the class teacher had planned a lesson in which the support teacher had no role.

CURRICULUM AND ORGANISATION

Key Stages 1, 2 and 3: Special Schools

17. All the special schools continued to support the principle of pupils' entitlement to full access to the National Curriculum. None of the special schools inspected had pupils with statements which disapplied any part of the National Curriculum.

18. Each school had undertaken at least some curriculum review, and just over a quarter of the schools had a well-documented curriculum which reflected National Curriculum Programmes of Study and Attainment Targets. A third of the schools had curriculum documents which only reflected National Curriculum Attainment Targets, and some 40 per cent had poor curriculum documentation, requiring considerable improvements. In general, progress in producing curriculum documents over the year was significantly slower than proposals and enthusiasm noted in the Autumn term visits had promised.

19. In most special schools the implementation of the National Curriculum had undoubtedly contributed to the provision of a broader and more balanced curriculum. However, almost half the sample had not yet achieved this. Limitations in curricular breadth and balance arose from the use of poorly-planned and unco-ordinated topics or themes some of which failed to cover science, history and geography adequately, and from the inadequate amount of time allocated to some foundation subjects. For example, in almost all the special schools where MFL teaching was inspected, the time allocated was between 30 and 60 minutes per week. This was significantly less than the time given to the subject at Key Stage 3 in ordinary secondary schools. Sometimes the MFL work in special schools was taught in one session per week because of the need to use part-time teachers; this reduced the opportunity for necessary frequent

practice of the target language. Overall, satisfactory curricular breadth and balance were achieved in fewer than a third of all schools.

20. Almost all the schools had designated members of staff to be responsible for the development and co-ordination of National Curriculum subjects throughout the school. Many of these teachers had recently attended centrally funded National Curriculum in-service training (INSET) sessions relating to their subject responsibilities. In just over half the schools these teachers had a positive influence on some of the teaching of their designated subject. Where their influence was not effective, it was frequently because their deployment did not allow sufficient time to carry out their responsibilities and share their expertise.

Key Stages 1 and 2: Primary Schools

21. Only half the schools had a written policy statement relating to provision and practice for pupils with SEN, and not all these schools had the necessary strategies in place to implement and evaluate their policies.

22. All the schools had small numbers of pupils with statements and none of the statements specified any disapplication of the National Curriculum. In two-thirds of the schools all the pupils with SEN had access to a broad and balanced curriculum. In some areas the lack of breadth and balance in the curriculum for some pupils with SEN was because they were withdrawn from class groups for literacy support to an extent which caused them to miss work in other subjects. Where topic work was poorly co-ordinated, this also limited the breadth of the curriculum for the pupils.

23.   Most of the curriculum for pupils with SEN was taught within mixed ability class groups. In about a quarter of the schools the pupils with SEN were extracted from their class into small groups for some of their time for the purpose of receiving additional teaching in English and, to a lesser extent, mathematics. The quality of this teaching varied however and was not always of a standard sufficient to justify extraction from the mainstream classes.

24.   About half the schools provided for part of each week some additional teaching for pupils with SEN within mixed ability classes. In half the schools the teaching provided as in-class support was jointly planned and co-ordinated with the work of the class teacher. Some 60 per cent of the schools had SSAs working with pupils with SEN. These SSAs were often specified as provision for pupils with statements. Where the work of the SSAs was well-planned to complement the work of the class teacher it made a very valuable contribution to a pupil's education.

25.   More than 50 per cent of the schools had designated a teacher as the co-ordinator for SEN. However, in 20 per cent of schools visited the post was filled by a teacher who had not completed a special educational needs in ordinary schools (SENIOS) training course of one term full-time or its part-time equivalent. Only about half of the co-ordinators had the skills and time to make a positive impact on the work with pupils with SEN throughout the school.

Key Stage 3: Secondary Schools

26.   More than two-thirds of the secondary schools had written policy statements detailing provision and practice for pupils with SEN but only half these schools had put the policy into practice.

27. All the schools had some pupils with statements of SEN and in one school 5 per cent of the total had statements (this included pupils in unit provision who were integrated in mainstream classes for most of their time). None of the statements specified any disapplication of the National Curriculum.

28. In two-thirds of the schools, the pupils with SEN had full access to a balanced and broadly based curriculum, including all subjects of the National Curriculum. The major reason for a lack of breadth and balance in the curriculum for pupils with SEN in about a third of the schools was the over-use of withdrawal groups to provide additional English and, to a lesser extent, mathematics, and more specific help for those with severe literacy difficulties. Almost two-thirds of the schools also used additional teacher support within subject classes for pupils with SEN. However, only half this additional support was jointly planned and co-ordinated with the work of subject teachers to maximise the benefits of this provision. In half the schools there were SSA staff for designated pupils and, as in primary schools, only about half of their work was well planned and co-ordinated with the work of teachers. An alternative to withdrawal or in-class support was teaching SEN pupils in lower ability sets. Work in these lower sets was often more narrowly focused and less effective than that in the higher or mixed ability sets.

29. Almost all the schools had designated a teacher as co-ordinator for SEN and many of them had attended relevant in-service training courses. In over 60 per cent of the schools this teacher had a positive influence on the provision and the practice for pupils with SEN.

ASSESSMENT, RECORDING AND REPORTING

Key Stages 1, 2 and 3: Special Schools

30.   Review and change of the procedures for assessment, recording and reporting continued to be of concern to teachers, but progress was not yet satisfactory. Thirty per cent of the special schools had assessment and recording procedures which had some good features, but these did not always match National Curriculum requirements. Seventy-five per cent of the schools only recorded pupil progress in National Curriculum subjects by means of a termly record of Attainment Targets covered, with only 15 per cent using Statements of Attainments as part of their criteria for assessment of pupil progress. Fifteen per cent of schools had no effective whole-school policy or framework for assessment, recording and reporting. A similar proportion of schools had unco-ordinated procedures in which individual teachers maintained separate, often limited, records with no satisfactory information on pupil performance in National Curriculum subjects. The large majority of schools had quite detailed discussion with parents when their child's annual review occurred and within this the parents were being given an increasing amount of information about their child's performance in National Curriculum subjects.

Key Stages 1 and 2: Primary Schools

31.   All the primary schools were developing their assessment, recording and reporting procedures, and all were at least recording Levels on particular Attainment Targets for mathematics and English. In about half the schools there was evidence that National Curriculum assessment of pupils' performance was being used to plan and map out a progression in the work to match pupils' needs. Encouragingly, two of the schools had introduced Records of Achievement for all pupils.

Key Stage 3: Secondary Schools

32.   All the secondary schools were developing their procedures for assessment, recording and reporting. Subject departments were maintaining records of Levels for Attainment Targets which had been covered. However, working contacts were often poor between English department teachers and other staff teaching English to pupils with SEN in small support groups. It was not unusual to find two unco-ordinated record systems, with records of work done by pupils in small groups seldom containing information about pupil performance in National Curriculum terms. Some mathematics and science teachers were very critical of the early changes in the National Curriculum in these subjects, which had required changes in procedures only recently established. In a sample in which all the schools had some pupils with statements under the 1981 Act, most schools used the annual review* as an opportunity to inform parents about pupils' progress. In a few schools, though, the parents were not involved in the annual review of statements.

*Annual review: a procedure established under the 1981 Education Act which requires LEAs to review statements at least annually. Reviews should normally be based on reports prepared by the school the child attends and should include where appropriate the views of teachers and other professionals who work with the child, and the assessments made under the 1988 Act with reference to the National Curriculum.

Key Stages 1, 2 and 3: Special Schools

33.   In almost all the special schools, teaching staff numbers were at least satisfactory, in terms of the levels advised in DES Circular 11/90. In some schools the staffing was better than these levels. Few schools reported difficulties in recruiting teaching staff, but some 10 per cent had a high turnover of teachers and rather more than this reported frequent difficulties in obtaining staff for supply cover purposes. Over half the schools lacked a range of staff expertise sufficient to provide full coverage of the National Curriculum subjects. Particular shortages were noted in science, music and MFL. Some schools have not yet moved far enough into implementing the full National Curriculum subject range to be fully aware of their deficiencies in subject expertise. The match between initial qualifications and areas of responsibility was sometimes poor. In just over half the schools the numbers of SSAs in post were below those advised in the staffing circular.

34.   Almost all the special schools reported involvement in school-based INSET on a range of National Curriculum subjects in the past year, but only 60 per cent had taken part in National Curriculum INSET provided within their areas by LEAs or by higher education (HE) institutions. In some 20 per cent of the schools teachers criticised National Curriculum INSET provided by LEAs or HE institutions as lacking relevance to SEN.

Key Stages 1 and 2: Primary Schools

35.   All the schools had satisfactory teaching staff levels for the numbers of pupils and range of SEN in the schools. In a few schools the role of co-ordinator of SEN was filled by a teacher who had not completed special educational needs in ordinary schools training. An increasing proportion of schools reported difficulties in obtaining supply cover for teaching staff. One

school used an agency which although they felt was expensive at £150 per day, was found to be very reliable. In 20 per cent of the schools the number of SSAs in post was below the level for pupils with statements advised in DES Circular 11/90. It was clear that there were wide variations in the criteria used by different LEAs in deciding on the amount of SSA support for pupils with statements in ordinary schools.

36. All the schools reported they had been involved in school-based and externally-provided INSET for National Curriculum subjects in the past year. In almost 50 per cent of schools INSET arrangements generally, and for SEN in particular, were reported to be vulnerable or already reduced because of financial constraints in the LEAs, including the cutting of advisory teacher posts. SEN INSET was increasingly becoming dependent on school-based arrangements and on the schools' co-ordinators for SEN who, in many cases, had to face increasing demands on their time.

Key Stage 3: Secondary Schools

37. The vast majority of the secondary schools in the sample had satisfactory teaching staff and SSA levels for the numbers of pupils and range of SEN. However, even within these schools there were difficulties in providing enough SSA support in classrooms for the successful full integration of pupils with SEN. Difficulties in obtaining supply cover staff were reported in more than a quarter of the schools.

38. In all the schools, staff reported involvement in school-based and externally provided INSET for National Curriculum subjects in the past year, but several said that this did not take account of SEN issues. As in primary and special schools, cutbacks in INSET provided by the LEA were reported.

Special Schools

39.   In over a third of the schools there was a general shortage of space for the numbers on roll. Although there has been some reduction in the number of pupils in special schools, the groups of pupils identified as having moderate learning difficulties (MLD), severe learning difficulties (SLD) and emotional and behavioural difficulties (EBD) has not reduced. Some of these pupils are profoundly handicapped and require more space than was originally provided. In addition the inclusion of the National Curriculum into the curriculum of all special schools has made demands on the accommodation available in special schools. In a third of the schools there was inadequate specialist accommodation for science and technology. Altogether, deficiencies in accommodation restricted National Curriculum provision in just over half the schools.

40.   There were some shortages in equipment and resources which adversely affected the teaching of the National Curriculum in more than 50 per cent of schools. In a number of schools, capitation is based on an historical formula and is only now being revised to meet the requirements of the National Curriculum. In their attempts to implement the National Curriculum, almost half the schools made substantial use of voluntary funding. In 30 per cent of the schools there was a good level of provision of microcomputers and Technical and Vocational Education Initiative (TVEI) money had frequently been used to achieve this level of provision. The general level of book provision was satisfactory in about two-thirds of the schools. However, across the schools there were significant shortages of resources for technology, science, mathematics and English in all the Key Stages, which inhibited the implementation of these subjects and the effectiveness with which they were taught to pupils. More detailed curriculum planning is needed that includes the identification of resources for specific areas of work; such planning could help alleviate these weaknesses.

Key Stages 1 and 2: Primary Schools

41. More than a third of the primary schools had some deficiencies in the accommodation available for teaching their pupils with SEN, and a similar number were also in a poor state of decoration and general repair.

42. Many schools had not carried out a full audit of their equipment and resources. About a quarter of the schools were drawing on voluntary funding to supplement the funding of the implementation of the National Curriculum for pupils with SEN, and rather more than this had insufficient resources for these pupils. Book supply was unsatisfactory in about a third of cases and there were major shortages in technology, science and mathematics.

Key Stage 3: Secondary Schools

43. More than two-thirds of the secondary schools had suitable accommodation for the numbers and range of pupils with SEN. However, in more than a quarter of the schools the accommodation was in a poor state of general decoration and was in need of repair in some.

44. Equipment and resources for SEN were less than satisfactory in about half the schools. There were major shortages in resources in science, mathematics and English. In mathematics and English particularly, resources were often tied to the main school texts which were not always appropriate for pupils with SEN. In over 60 per cent of the schools the books and materials had not been chosen sufficiently carefully to provide the range necessary to help pupils with SEN. Where differentiation of materials was attempted it was often through the use of poorly devised worksheets. If school assessment procedures fail to adequately monitor the levels of ability at intake, the use of inappropriate resources will continue to inhibit the progress of pupils with SEN.

45. The findings of this report suggest that for progress to continue in implementing the National Curriculum for pupils with special educational needs, the following issues will need to be addressed:

- schools generally, and special schools in particular, should review and monitor their curricular provision to assess how well it provides the coverage and access for pupils with SEN, envisaged in the 1988 Education Act;

- to overcome the loss of momentum that seems to occur over the course of the school year, lesson planning in many schools needs to focus more carefully upon the National Curriculum Programmes of Study and Statements of Attainment and take account of assessments of pupils' performance in planning for progression;

- as for all pupils, the effective assessment of educational performance is of crucial importance for those with special educational needs. This remains a weak aspect of the work in many schools. Teachers can hardly expect to plan and provide a good match of work to ability and special needs in the absence of an assessment of pupils' performance which adequately pinpoints their strengths and weaknesses. This issue should be addressed more urgently in the provision of in-service training (INSET) and in the arrangements for assessing, recording and reporting of pupils' performance within the schools;

- unsuitable provision and gaps in the range of teaching resources and, to a lesser extent, accommodation for pupils with SEN present obstacles to their progress in some subjects in a significant number of schools. Schools need to conduct a thorough audit of provision of books and teaching materials for pupils with special educational needs, and take account of the improvements required in the school development plan. Many schools could also achieve a better match of work to the pupils' developing abilities, for example, by designing worksheets and home-made materials more carefully and adjusting their purchasing policies to provide a better range of printed materials, including books;

- it is disappointing to find that the additional support provided by a SSA is sometimes wasted. On the other hand, where such support is planned and co-ordinated in ways that complement the work of the teacher, the benefits to the pupils with SEN can be enormous.

Should We Stay or Should We Go?
Two Views on Britain and the EU

Lord Pearson of Rannoch
Stephen Pollard

Civitas: Institute for the Study of Civil Society
London

First published May 2005

© The Institute for the Study of Civil Society 2005
77 Great Peter Street
London SW1P 2EZ
email: books@civitas.org.uk

ISBN 1-903 386-40 3

Typeset by Civitas

in Palatino

Printed in Great Britain by
St Edmundsbury Press
Bury St Edmunds, Suffolk IP33 3TZ

Contents

Authors

Malcolm Pearson founded the PWS Group of international insurance brokers in 1964. He was raised to the peerage in 1990 and since 1992 has been a leading exponent in the Lords of the case for the UK to leave the EU. In 1998, with Lord Harris of High Cross and Lord Stoddart of Swindon, he founded Global Britain, a non-party think tank, to research alternatives to UK membership of the European Union.

Stephen Pollard is a columnist who writes regularly in *The Times, Sunday Telegraph, Independent* and *Wall Street Journal Europe* about politics, policy and culture. He is a Senior Fellow at the Centre for the New Europe, the Brussels-based free market think tank, where he directs the health policy programme, and at Civitas. In February 2005 he was an expert witness in the US Senate's hearing on drug importation. He is co-author with Andrew Adonis (now the Prime Minister's senior policy adviser) of the best-selling *A Class Act: the myth of Britain's classless society* (1998). His biography of David Blunkett was published in December 2004.

Foreword

The majority of people in Britain have doubts about the proposed EU constitution, but not all want to leave the EU altogether. This publication compares two views about our relationship with the European Union. Stephen Pollard is opposed to the constitution but wants to remain in the EU. He accepts that there is a strong case for fundamental reform, but believes that it will be possible to find allies for change among the other 24 countries. Lord Pearson argues that the EU is beyond reform and that the UK should leave. Its main governing institutions are undemocratic and lacking in accountability; it has an inclination to over-regulate and thus tie our hands as we struggle to compete with emerging economies elsewhere in the world; and its protectionism undermines the efforts of poor countries to flourish through trade.

Some of our books are designed for the academic world and some are designed for a wider readership. *Should We Stay Or Should We Go?* is polemical in the best sense of that term: it is a controversial disputation that allows trenchantly argued rival views to be compared. By presenting two contrasting views our intention is for the book to be valuable to teachers in schools and universities where students are encouraged to evaluate the issues for themselves.

David G. Green

Better Off Out!

A brief summary of our relationship with 'Brussels',
including the case for the United Kingdom to leave the EU
and the case to stay.

Lord Pearson of Rannoch

A. *Our democracy betrayed*

'Sovereignty', the 'British Constitution', our 'democracy', 'self-government'; what threads run through these priceless things, and hold them together? At least two fundamental principles are common to all of them. The first is the hard-won right of the British people to elect and dismiss those who make their laws. The second is that the British people have given Parliament the power to make all their laws for them, but they have not given Parliament permission to give that power away.

Both these principles, for which, over the centuries, millions have willingly given up their lives, already stand deeply betrayed by our membership of the European Union. I propose to justify this depressing statement under three headings.

First, what is the present position under the Treaties of Rome; how much of our democracy have we already handed over to the corrupt octopus in Brussels and how were we deceived into doing it? Second, how much is this costing us in cash and is it worth it? And third, what does the proposed EU Constitution have in store for us?

It is essential to remember that the peoples' pact is with Parliament; it is not with the executive or government of the day. The people elect and dismiss Members of Parliament once every four or five years, and our government is formed out of a majority of elected MPs. But only 60 per cent of the electorate now bother to vote in general elections, and

1

modern governments are supported by only some 40 per cent of those who do vote, or 24 per cent of the electorate. The percentage of those who vote is declining; trust in our system of parliamentary democracy is eroding steadily. I submit therefore that these temporary governments, always empowered by a minority of the people, do not have the right to break the great pacts upon which our sovereignty rests. Yet that is just what they have been doing for the last 33 years.

B. How bad is it now and how does it work?

So, first, how bad is the present situation? Few people realise what huge areas of our national life have already been handed over to control by Brussels. Put simply, these include all of our commerce and industry, our social and labour policy, our environment, agriculture, fish, and foreign aid.

What do we mean by 'control from Brussels'? Well, in all those areas of our national life, which used to be entirely controlled by Parliament, our government can be outvoted in the Council of Ministers from the member states, where it has nine per cent of the votes. You need 30 per cent to block a new law. That is the system known as Qualified Majority Voting, or QMV. If our government is outvoted on any new law in those areas, then Parliament, being the House of Commons and the Lords, must put it into British law. If they don't, the country faces unlimited fines in the Luxembourg Court of Justice.[1] So Parliament has already become a rubber stamp in all those areas.

Our foreign trade relations are in an even worse category. The EU bureaucracy, the Commission, itself negotiates those on our behalf,[2] and so in this area the EU already has its own legal personality (to which I shall return).

In addition, laws affecting our 'justice and home affairs', and our 'foreign and security policy', must also be rubber-stamped by Parliament if they have been agreed by our government and all the other member states' governments in Brussels.[3] In other words, our government can still veto new laws in Brussels in these areas of our national life, but if they don't, we have to enact them. If Parliament were to reject an EU law thus agreed in Brussels in these areas, we would not be subject to unlimited fines in the Luxembourg Court, but we would be in breach of our Treaty obligations, which is an equally horrifying prospect to our political classes at their diplomatic cocktail parties and so on.

There is no appeal against the Luxembourg Court. This is not a court of law, but rather the engine of the Treaties. It must find in favour of *'the ever closer union of the peoples of Europe'*,[4] and it interprets the Treaties with much laxity in order to do so.

The Government admits that over half our major laws, and 80 per cent of all laws, now originate in Brussels.[5] No law passed in Brussels has ever been successfully overturned by Parliament.

There are at least four other features of this Brussels system which are worth emphasising, all of them innately undemocratic.

First, the unelected and corrupt bureaucracy, the Commission, has the monopoly to propose all new laws.[6] They simply can't believe that in Washington.

Second, the Commission's legal proposals are then negotiated in secret by the shadowy Committee of Permanent Representatives, or bureaucrats from the nation states, known as COREPER. Decisions are taken in the Council of Ministers, again by secret vote. Even national parliaments are precluded from knowing how their bureaucrats or ministers negotiate and vote, and few details of the continuous horse-trading leak out to the general public. The Commission then enforces all EU law.

The Eurocrats pretend that democracy is maintained because decisions are taken in the Council by national ministers, who were elected as national MPs. But the point remains that Parliament itself is excluded from the process, except as a rubber stamp when the decisions have been taken. Examples of how we have suffered under this system are too numerous to mention, but there is for instance the

'Young People at Work' Directive, which hit our paper rounds, and the Working Time Directive, which is now haunting our National Health Service.

The Government could have vetoed the infamous EU Arrest Warrant because it was proposed under 'Justice and Home Affairs'. This allows British subjects to be extradited, purely on the say-so of a foreign EU magistrate, to stand trial in that magistrate's country, without the benefit of *habeas corpus* or a jury, perhaps for crimes which are not even crimes in the UK—such as 'xenophobia', for which we don't even have a legal definition (but I expect I'm committing it now!). The decision to proceed with that particularly pernicious piece of EU legislation went through on the nod in the Council of Ministers. The then Home Secretary, David Blunkett, did not utter a single word, because the whole project had already been stitched up in COREPER. So much for even the shallowest pretence at real democracy.

Please don't be fooled by the propaganda which says that Parliament can scrutinise and debate EU legislation. Indeed we do, until the cows come home, but we cannot change a comma of it unless that change is unanimously agreed by all the member states in the Council of Ministers. This is entirely unrealistic and indeed no such changes have ever even been suggested by Parliament. We also debate and vote on each new EU Treaty, but again we cannot change a word. We either accept the whole thing, or we reject it all. So Parliament has always accepted every Treaty precisely as agreed in Brussels, even if some of us have forced votes against them in protest.

A third feature of this awful system, enshrined in the Treaties, is that once an area of national life has been ceded to control from Brussels, it can never be returned to national parliaments.[7] This is known in Euro-speak as the '*Acquis Communautaire*' or 'powers acquired by the Community'. In plain English this translates as the 'ratchet', which can only grind in one direction toward the 'ever closer union of the peoples of Europe'.

The fourth feature is that no changes can be made to the Treaties unless they are agreed unanimously in the Council of Ministers.[8] So renegotiation of the Treaties is not realistic; the only way out is the door.

For good measure, we should remember that the EU is corrupt and corrupting from top to bottom. Its own internal auditors have refused to sign its accounts for the last nine years. No fewer than five whistleblowers have been side-lined in the last five years. The problem is that there is no European demos, so there can be no European democracy to hold the fraudsters and free-loaders to account. The MEPs are supposed to sort the Commission out in this area, but their own travel and office expenses are famously bogus. The MEPs are also far too frightened of bringing the EU into further disrepute to fulfill their duty to the taxpayer. They would risk bringing the whole gravy train to a halt, or they might be pushed off it; most of them are unemployable elsewhere, certainly at anything like their present salaries and 'conditions'.

It's also worth saying that the whole of continental Europe will continue in steady and irreversible demographic and therefore economic decline over the next 50 years.[9] The UK and Ireland will improve their demography, as of course will Turkey. The USA also looks healthy, Japan looks terrible, China and the Far East are set to boom. Add to this the unemployment and decay caused by the EU's adoption of Franco-German social and labour policies, and you have to ask: 'Why stay on the Titanic?'

So those are the huge areas of our sovereignty we have already given away. That's why giving away most of what is left, under the proposed new EU Constitution, is described by the Government as a 'tidying-up' exercise. They have a point. The Constitution would merely sweep most of what is left under the Brussels carpet.

C. History: how did we get into this mess?

The European 'Project' was the brain-child of a British civil servant, Arthur Salter, at the end of the First World War. He was assisted by a young Frenchman, Jean Monnet.

The Project re-emerged after the Second World War and its fundamental idea was (and, believe it or not, still is), that nation states were responsible for the carnage of two World Wars. They must therefore be emasculated, and diluted into a supra-national state, run by a Commission of wise and honest technocrats. Hence the Commission's monopoly to propose legislation. So the 'Project' confuses dangerous nationalism with honourable patriotism.

Most of us reject conspiracy theories, but the EU Project is indeed a massive deception of the people by the political élite of Europe. Anyone who doubts this should read a brilliant book by Christopher Booker and Richard North, entitled *The Great Deception*, which reveals the detailed history of how the people have been misled. The authors have unearthed several internal Foreign Office memos under the 30-year rule. There is one beauty from a senior civil servant in 1971 to a colleague, who acknowledged that it meant the end of British democracy as it had been previously understood, but if properly handled the people would not realise what had happened until the end of the century.[10]

I have space to expose only one proof of this terrible deception, by quoting a filleted extract of Sections 2 and 3 of the European Communities Act 1972, which is the Act which took us into what was then the European Common Market. It goes as follows:

> All such rights, powers, liabilities, obligations and restrictions from time to time created or arising by or under the Treaties ... are without further enactment to be given legal effect ... and be enforced, allowed and followed accordingly.

> Subject to Schedule 2 to this Act, at any time after its passing Her Majesty may by Order in Council, and any designated Minister or department may by regulations, make provision ... for the purpose of implementing any Community obligation of the United Kingdom.

Section 3 reads as follows:

> For the purposes of all legal proceedings, any question as to the meaning or effect of any of the Treaties, or as to the validity, meaning or effect of any Community instrument, shall be treated as a question of law (and, if not referred to the European Court, be for determina-

tion as such in accordance with the principles laid down by and any relevant decision of the European Court).

Articles 226-229 of the Treaty Establishing the European Communities (TEC) give the Luxembourg Court the right to impose unlimited fines if we don't obey everything agreed in Brussels.

Yet Edward Heath had the nerve to promise that 'no loss of essential sovereignty' was involved in the passing of the 1972 Act. Harold Wilson said the same thing during the 1975 Referendum campaign. Both Prime Ministers pretended we had merely joined a Common Market. I fear Margaret Thatcher was deceived as to the way the Single European Act of 1986 would be used, which created the system of Qualified Majority Voting. She bitterly regrets it today, as is well-known. John Major then misled us about the Maastricht Treaty of 1992, and Tony Blair misled us over the Amsterdam Treaty of 1997 and the Nice Treaty of 2002. It has always been essential to keep the true nature of the Project from the British people. They have to be slowly sucked into the embrace of the corrupt octopus, until it is too late to escape. That is the very essence of the Project, and so far it is working pretty well.

D. How much does EU membership cost us in cash?[11]

The Government steadfastly refuses to carry out any sort of cost-benefit analysis, although my friends and I in the Lords have made several attempts to force it to do so (see our debates 27 June 2003 and 11 February 2004). Ministers merely insist that the benefits of our EU membership are so obvious and wonderful that any analysis would be a waste of time and money. Presumably the Government doesn't want the following sort of figures to see the light of day.

D(i) Annual Costs:

If we start by looking at annual expenditure, we very easily reach an annual waste of some £40 billion pounds a year. A billion pounds, one thousand million pounds, is a rather confusing figure, and most people don't stop to think what it means. Well, one thousand million pounds builds, equips and staffs a decent district hospital to run indefinitely. You build and equip it for £80 - £100 million, and then you have a fund of £900 million to run it. So perhaps we should measure our Euro-waste in district hospitals, rather than billions, but I'll go back to billions for now.

According to the Trade Justice Movement, supported by CAFOD and Oxfam, the EU's Common Agricultural Policy (CAP) costs each family of four in the UK about £20 a week, or a fiver a head. Half of this is incurred through higher food costs (against what we would pay for the same food on the open world market) and half through the higher taxes we pay to keep EU farmers in the style to which they have become accustomed. The higher food costs work out at approximately 5p on a pint of milk, 40p on a 60p bag of sugar, and 3p on a loaf of bread. So these costs hit the poorest in our society hardest, and total about £15.6 billion every year. The EU's charming policy of dumping its unwanted excess produce on the developing world also starves untold numbers to death, mostly children, because local farmers can't sell their produce in local markets.

The Dutch Government has calculated that EU over-regulation costs the Dutch economy some two per cent of their Gross Domestic Product annually.[12] It is fair to assume that EU overregulation doesn't cost the UK economy any less than it costs the Dutch, given Whitehall's well-known practice of 'gold-plating' EU legislation. Our GDP is around £1,000 billion, and so two per cent of that would come to £20 billion annually.

Then there's the hard cash we hand over to Brussels every year. Over the last ten years we have given Brussels an average of £11 billion per annum to help them finance the whole vast swindle. Of this, they have been good enough to send back to us an average of some £7 billion annually, always for projects here which are designed to enhance their wretched image (including the CAP). So that leaves £4 billion straight cash outflow per annum.[13]

There are lots of other areas which could be thrown into this calculation, such as at least £1 billion p.a. for the destruction of our fishing industry, and another billion for the ruin of our modern art market, and so on. But just sticking to the figures I have mentioned, we have a comfortable 40 district hospitals chucked away every year.

Let's examine that figure, £40 billion per annum, a little further, shall we? It comes to £110 million a day, £5 million per hour, or £666 per annum for each one of us. It is ten times our railways budget, which Heaven knows could do with a bit of a boost. It is three times our whole transport budget. It is two-thirds of our education budget, and it is ten district hospitals per annum more than our entire defence budget, which weighs in at a mere £27 billion per annum.[14]

So that's a conservative estimate of how much our EU membership is costing us in cash each year: £40 billion. What about some of the longer-term projects which we pay for, courtesy of the Eurocrats in Brussels?

D (ii) Capital Projects

The last time the Government dared to answer my Written Questions in the Lords, some three years ago, we had already spent £48 billion on the pointless water directives —there was nothing wrong with our water before. Then there's £18 billion so far on the outdated Euro-fighter; £8 billion on the foot and mouth saga (which was directed from Brussels); another £8 billion for removing the harmless kind of asbestos from our buildings; £6 billion for 'Reach', the new chemical analysis Directive, and yet another £6 billion for the Waste Electrical and Equipment Directive, which is starting to cause dumping in the countryside. I could go on, but that's another 94 district hospitals so far.

E. The case for staying in the EU

Surely there must be good things we get out of our EU membership? Well, I will try to set out the case for staying in the EU, as put forward by the Government and other Europhiles in our most recent Lords debates, to which I have referred (27 June 2003 and 11 February 2004). Presumably it's the best case they can make.

If you read those debates, you will see that there isn't really a case for the EU. It just isn't possible to identify any genuine benefits we have had from our EU membership, which we couldn't have had under simple free trade arrangements and collaboration between governments. But I will do my best. The propaganda runs as follows:

1. *'60 per cent of our trade and three million jobs depend on our membership of the EU'*. This is designed to fool the British people into fearing that they cannot afford to leave the EU. Not true. By the word *'trade'*, they actually mean *'exports of manufactured goods'* which account for less than half of total UK exports. But since Brussels' dictats apply to and strangle 100 per cent of our economy, the only way to understand the effect of our EU membership is to look at the whole of our output and all our jobs. Then we see the true picture, which is that only about ten per cent of our output and jobs support our trade with the EU, another ten per cent goes in trade with the rest of the world, and the remaining 80 per cent stays right here in our domestic market.[15] Our healthy 90 per cent dog is being wagged by its mangy ten per cent tail.

Not that the ten per cent of our output and jobs which support our trade with the EU are unimportant. No-one is saying that. But the obvious fact is that we would not lose that ten per cent of output or jobs if we left the EU and continued our free trade with the Single Market. And there really isn't any doubt that that is what we would do. The EU trades in massive surplus with the UK. They sell us far more than we sell them. This means they have many more jobs dependent on their trade with us than we do on our trade with them. We are by far their largest client. So if we left the EU, they would come running after us to make sure we signed a free trade agreement with them. After all, Switzerland, Mexico and 20 other countries already enjoy free trade agreements with the EU, which is negotiating FTAs with a further 69 countries.[16] This makes 91 countries in all, about half the countries in the world. So if we left the EU we could maintain all our present trading arrangements, plus no doubt 'free movement of persons' and so on, which again Switzerland already enjoys. We could dictate our terms.

Even free trade with the EU is no longer such a big deal as it used to be. The World Trade Organisation has brought the EU's average external tariff—paid by the US and most other countries in the world to export into the EU—down to about 1.5 per cent.[17] Indeed, every major economic study this century agrees that leaving the EU would be at worst neutral for our trade and jobs. The leftish and fairly Europhile National Institute of Social and Economic Research said that in March 2000.[18] The International Trade Commission in Washington, perhaps the world's largest and most prestigious economic think-tank, said it in a report to Congress in August 2000.[19] Our Institute of Economic Affairs said it in 1996 and again in 2002.[20] Even Neil Kinnock and the EU Trade Commissioner, Fritz Bolkestein, were forced to admit it on BBC Radio 4's Today programme in February 2001. In fact, no-one except the Europhile propagandists pretends that leaving the EU would bring economic disadvantage to the people of Great Britain. Our trade would continue, and so would our jobs.

It is encouraging that the British people appear to have understood this point. The latest opinion poll, published in *The Times* on 23 November 2004, showed that 68 per cent of people between the ages of 18 and 24, and 65 per cent over all age groups, would vote to reduce our relationship with the EU to one of simple free trade. These percentages fall considerably when pollsters ask if respondents want to leave the EU, although reducing our relationship to simple free trade would in fact mean leaving the Treaties.

2. *'We gain influence by sharing our sovereignty. Look at NATO and the United Nations. We gave up sovereignty to join them.'*
Answer: Sovereignty is like virginity. You either have it or

you don't. NATO and the UN don't dictate most of our unwanted laws and regulations, and we could leave them tomorrow if we felt like it.

3. We are told that *'the British people voted to join the EU in the referendum of 1975'* and so that should be the end of the matter. But they didn't. They voted to stay in what they were assured was a Common Market, or free trade area.

4. They claim that *'if we left the EU we would still have to obey all its rules, but not be able to participate in making those rules'*. Not so. The truth is that those who make up the ten per cent of our economy which exports to the EU would of course have to meet Brussels' requirements, as does every other non-EU exporter from the rest of the world, just as it pays to put the steering wheel on the left if you are selling a car to the US market. But the other 90 per cent of our economy would no longer have to obey the dictats from Brussels. Exports to the EU from the USA and Switzerland, who are not EU members, are going up faster than those from any of the member states.[21]

5. *'Our membership of the EU makes us the gateway for inward investment into Europe'*. Nonsense. Foreigners invest here because of our reliable workforce, low tax and regulatory régime (until the EU destroys that), and because we speak English. Surprisingly, there is little evidence that inward investment creates many jobs anyway, and 80 per cent of it goes into oil, gas and services which do not supply EU markets.[22]

6. Then there's the claim that *our bond market, the City of London, and so on, would all collapse if we left the EU*. That's what they told us would happen if we didn't join the euro. The greatest threat to the City and our bond market actually came from the EU, with its withholding tax proposals, which even Gordon Brown threatened to veto.

7. We are told that if we Eurosceptics would only shut up, *the UK could take its place at the heart of 'Europe' and lead it into the paths of righteousness*; that the French and the Germans

would somehow abandon their ruinous social and labour policies, instead of forcing them on the rest of us through the Single Market. But how can we persuade them of our national interest, with only nine per cent of the votes? Why have we been unable to change even the notorious Common Agricultural and Fisheries Policies in the 32 years of our membership?

8. They say *'the EU must be good news because ten new Eastern European nations have voted to join it'*. The answers here are that, first, turnout in all the referenda was very low. Second, the people weren't told the truth about the EU; most of them weren't told about the proposed new Constitution at all. Third, the spending by the 'Yes' sides was massively more than the 'No' sides. In Estonia, for instance, the 'Yes' campaign spent 60 times what the 'No' campaign could raise. But most important of all, the key to understanding the 'Yes' votes is that most of the bureaucrats and politicians who negotiated the entry of their countries into the EU stand to get jobs in Brussels, or be paid on the EU scale. The Polish ambassador has told me that 1,400 Poles will now get EU jobs, at ten times their present salaries.

9. We're told that *the EU Project is 're-uniting Europe'*. But if you ask them when Europe was last 'united' in the way they wish to see it 're-united', you get a rather uncomfortable look. (Caesar? Napoleon? Hitler?)

10. *'The EU is a success.'* Only for those who make money out of it!

11. This leads me to perhaps the most effective piece of Europhile propaganda: *that the EU has secured the peace in Europe since 1945, and is essential to maintain it in future.* This is the big deception which plays at the almost unconscious level. It is a warm, misty conviction that the EU must be inevitably good. It does not tolerate any rational examination of history or the facts. It's the one which makes those of us who query the divinity of the EU Project into dangerous nationalists, xenophobes, Little Englanders, or worse. You

start to be guilty of all this as soon as you dare to point out that NATO was entirely responsible for keeping the peace in Europe until the Wall came down in 1989, or if you ask which European country would have gone to war with another in the absence of the EU. So even this essential plank of Euro-propaganda is simply wishful thinking, constantly repeated by the Eurocrats in order to justify their bloated lifestyles and the Project in general.

Indeed, if you stand back, scratch your head a bit, and take a calm look at the EU, you see it is a well-tried model for discord, not peace. It contains two of the most important ingredients for conflict.

First, it is a top-down amalgamation of different peoples, put together without their informed consent, and such arrangements usually end in conflict. You only have to look at Northern Ireland, Yugoslavia, the Trans-Caucasus, Kashmir and most of Africa to see that.

Second, as I have pointed out, the EU is institutionally undemocratic. It is also corrupt, which is another ingredient for trouble. I repeat, the Project aims to replace 'dangerous' national democracies with a supra-national government, run by a Commission of wise and honest technocrats. But history shows us that on the whole democracies do not provoke war, and indeed its hard to think of a genuine democracy which has declared war on another. So Euro-sceptics believe that a free trade association between the democracies of Europe, linked through NATO, is much less likely to end in tears than is the emerging undemocratic mega-state.

12. Whilst on the subject of peace, I should mention that a new *raison d'être* is coming to the surface in Brussels. A large majority of Eurocrats and Europhiles see the EU's main purpose in life as being to stand up to and undermine the United States of America. In fact, this was always part of the Project, inspired by France's deep psychotic need to bite the hand that freed her in two World Wars. Luckily, there is little prospect that the EU will be able to provide the

defence budget necessary to fulfill this ambition, but it will continue to poison the trans-Atlantic relationship for the foreseeable future.

F. The euro

You may notice that I have said nothing about the euro, the single currency, which is an essential part of the Project, but which is off our national agenda for the time being. I have space to deal only with its worst aspects. First, it is not an economic project at all. It was always a purely political project, designed as the cement to hold the emerging EU megastate together. It also has serious design faults. The eurozone has no common language, its mobility of labour is low, and its single interest rate cannot suit 12 different and diverging economies for long. Above all, no currency can endure unless taxes are paid from rich to poor regions within its area (e.g. South to North in the UK; West to East in Germany; North to South in Italy; the federal budget in the USA). There is no federal budget to speak of in the EU, and of course the plan has always been to set one up in response to the stress which will therefore occur in the euro-zone. No prizes for guessing who will be in charge, or what this would do to our tax rates if we join.

G. What does the proposed new Constitution have in store for us?

The worst feature of this Constitution is that the EU will acquire its own legal personality, superior to that of the member states. There is no longer even the pretence that the EU is an arrangement between sovereign nations. The EU, the Brussels system, becomes Sovereign. The EU flag, which at the moment is flown as mere advertising, becomes real. The EU anthem becomes the anthem of the new mega-state. (Alas, poor Beethoven!)

The Prime Minister claims that he defended his 'red lines' at the Inter-Governmental Conference on 18 June 2004[23] which decided the Constitution's final shape. These include foreign policy, social security and tax. But large chunks of these areas have in fact already been ceded to the Treaties. For instance, Mr Blair's red line on tax is clearly a red herring. If you look at the tax provisions of the Treaties (Clause 93 of the Treaty Establishing the European Communities) you see that we have indeed retained the veto for indirect taxation. The Treaties are silent on direct taxation as such, but if you look at the single market provisions (Clauses 43 and 44) you will see that all direct tax is exposed to the 'anti-discrimination' and 'right of establishment' provisions. In other words, the Commission could claim that our direct tax system gives us an unfair advantage over the other member states. When the Court agreed, we would have to fall into line. It is a little known fact that the Court has already moved into corporation tax, and has issued some 90 judgements, usually against nation states keeping control of multi-national companies' dividend policy, etc.[24]

M. Giscard D'Estaing, who drafted the proposed Constitution, has done us all one great favour. The wording of the document is really very easy to understand; it is not written in the usual impenetrable verbiage of the Treaties. Anyone who takes the trouble to read it can understand it. Even so, there is one attempt at Euro-deception. The Constitution introduces the concepts of 'Exclusive Competences' and 'Shared Competences'. 'Competence' itself is an old Euro-deceptive word. It does not mean being able to do something well. It means 'power', and it usually means power transferred to the EU, where of course it is always exercised incompetently, and corruptly. So the Exclusive Competences are clear enough; the EU alone can act in those areas of our national life which are transferred to the EU's Exclusive Competence (mostly concerning competition, customs and the power to make international treaties). The deception lies in the 'Shared Competences', where you could be forgiven for thinking that power might be shared with the member states. Not a bit of it. Member states can only act in areas covered by 'Shared Competence' when Brussels can't be bothered, and with Brussels' permission.

These 'Shared Competences' are pretty wide. They include the internal market, which covers all of our commerce and industry; the 'area of freedom, security and justice'—so our immigration, asylum, legal system and judicial procedures will gradually pass to Brussels' control; our agriculture and fisheries (of course); all European transport and 'trans-european networks'; our energy (bang goes our oil and gas); social policy; 'economic, social and territorial cohesion'— which will mean almost anything when the Luxembourg Court gets going; our environment; consumer protection; and 'common safety concerns in public health matters'. Not much left, you might think.[25]

Sitting astride and above all this is not only the superior legal power of the new Union. There is also the fact that the EU's Charter of Fundamental Rights will be all embracing and justiciable in the Luxembourg Court. Even the Europhile Confederation of British Industry is worried about what the new right to strike, etc. will do for our international competitiveness.

The Eurocrats pretend that the Constitution returns power to national parliaments because the Commission has to reconsider a new law if one-third of national parliaments don't like it. But the Commission can go ahead anyway, so this is no big deal.

When we come to debate the Constitution, we really mustn't fall for one of the best tricks up the Eurocrat's sleeve. The trick is to proclaim that some feature of the Constitution is 'nothing new' because it is already in the Treaties, as though that makes it acceptable to the British people. It doesn't. If much of our sovereignty has been taken away when we weren't looking, that should not stop us from demanding it back, now that we have discovered what has been going on.

H. The Conservative Party and 'Europe'

Michael Howard has promised that a Conservative Government will 're-negotiate' the return of our fish. If the others don't agree, he will legislate in the House of Commons to take them back. This is the cunning plan of those many Conservatives who want to leave the EU, but don't dare to say so. Spain and Holland, at least, could not afford to lose our fish, so they would challenge their repatriation in Luxembourg. The Court would have to declare the UK's action unlawful, and we would then be faced with climbing down or leaving the EU. The Conservatives' other plan is to refuse to ratify the new Constitution, having won the eventual referendum, and allow the others to go ahead, but only in return for the repatriation of (unspecified) powers. This is less cunning, because the Treaties already allow eight or more other nations to *'enhance their co-operation'*, even if we disagree.[26] One cannot help wondering why the Conservatives don't simply move to a 'come-out' policy, merge with UKIP, and win the next general election. Their biggest problem is that they are stuck with their mantra: *'the single market is our greatest achievement in the EU.'* Yet it is single market legislation which does most of the damage to our economy. There will be no compromise with UKIP until the Conservatives come clean on that. They would also have to explain why they took us into the Project in the first place; and politicians are not good at public confession.

I. A couple of EU jokes

I suppose it's time for a couple of jokes about our EU membership, the only two I know. The first is that we shouldn't go on saying that we are 'giving' our sovereignty away; we are actually paying Brussels tens of billions of pounds a year to take it. The second is that if the EU applied to join itself, it wouldn't have a hope of being accepted, given its clear lack of democracy (the 'democratic deficit' in Eurospeak).

J. Conclusion—better off out

To conclude, we 'Eurosceptics' love the real Europe, the Europe of separate democracies, each with its glorious history and culture. But we fear the Project of European Union, which we see as a bad idea. It is a bad idea like slavery, communism and high rise flats. We must not forget the damage which ideas can do when they become generally accepted, but turn out to be wrong. I don't know if you have heard of the letter written by the young White Russian officer in 1918 to his fiancée from the front against the Bolsheviks: 'Oh, my darling! Please do not worry. In a few weeks I shall be home with you in Moscow, and we shall be married. These people are not very well armed, and their ideas are even worse.' A few days later he was killed, so he was wrong about their arms. But he turned out to be right about the ideas which inspired Soviet Communism. It is just that it took 70 years and 50 million lives to prove his point. Let's hope the EU doesn't end up as quite such a dangerous idea as that. With any luck it will start to decay from within, if we have the energy to understand it, expose it, and fight it.

There is nothing right-wing, negative, frightening or extreme about leaving the EU and keeping our hard-won right to govern ourselves. As the fourth biggest economy in the world, as its third largest trading nation,[27] and as a major military power, leaving the EU would be a liberating, refreshing, positive, modern thing to do. And we would be very much richer as well!

Better Off Out!

1 As per the Treaty Establishing the European Communities, or TEC.

2 Article 133, TEC.

3 As per the Treaty on European Union, or TEU (also known as the 'Maastricht Treaty').

4 Article 1, TEU.

5 Cabinet Office web-site: www.cabinet-office.gov.uk. April 2004.

6 Articles 211 and 249-254 of the TEC.

7 Articles 2, 3 & 6.4 of the TEU; and Protocol 30 of the TEC.

8 Article 48 TEU.

9 See, for example, Colombani, P., *Le Commerce Mondial au 21e siécle: Scénarios pour L'Union Européenne*, Institut Français des Relations Internationales, November 2002, www.ifri.org. Also Baroness Cox, House of Lords *Hansard*, 27 June 2003, Cols 540-543.

10 Booker, C. and North, R., *The Great Deception*, Continuum Books, 2003, p. 144, note 46. (Or see PRO/FCO/30/1048 [1971] undated)

11 And see groundbreaking new study by Milne, I., *A Cost Too Far?* London: Civitas, July 2004. www.civitas.org.uk.

12 Speech by Dutch Vice Prime Minister and Finance Minister, Mr Gerrit Zalm, to the UK Government- sponsored conference 'Advancing Enterprise: Britain in a Global Economy', 26 January 2004.

13 *UK Balance of Payments: The Pink Book 2003*, Office for National Statistics. www.statistics.gov.uk.

14 HM Treasury, Budget Statement, 17 March 2004, HC 301. www.hm- treasury.gov.uk.

15 Table 2.1: Supply & Use Tables for the United Kingdom, in *United Kingdom National Accounts: The Blue Book 2003*, Office for National Statistics 2001. www.statistics.gov.uk. Summarised in Global Britain Briefing Note No 22, *Ninety per cent of the British economy is NOT involved in exports to the EU*, 20th September 2002. www.globalbritain.org.

16 Written Answers, House of Lords, 5 July 2004 (HL 3440 and 3441).

17 See, for example, Global Britain Briefing Note No 33, *Customs Duties: Hardly Worth Collecting*, 17 September 2004, www.globalbritain.org.

18 Pain, N. and Young, G., *Continent Cut Off? The Macroeconomic Impact of British Withdrawal from the EU*, National Institute of Economics and Social Research (NIESR), February 2000.

19 *The Impact on the US Economy of Including the UK in a Free Trade Arrangement with the USA, Canada and Mexico*, International Trade Commission, Investigation No. 332-409, Publication No. 3339, August 2000. www.usitc.gov.

20 Hindley, B. and Howe, M., *Better Off Out?*, London: IEA, 1996 and 2001. www.iea.org.uk.

21 See, *Geographical Breakdown of the EU Current Account*, Eurostat/European Commission, 2002 edn. Summarised in Global Britain Briefing Note No. 27, *Single Market: USA Main Beneficiary*, 6 June 2003. www.globalbritain.org.

22 See, Milne, *A Cost Too Far?*, Chap. 6, 'The Importance of Inward Investment to the UK Economy', 2004. www.civitas.org.uk.

23 18 June was chosen because it is the anniversary of the Battle of Waterloo. (No more wars in Europe, thanks to the EU.)

24 See, House of Lords, *Hansard*, 25 February 2004, cols 313-328.

25 The proposed EU Constitution. CM 6289. www.fco.gov.uk. For indexed version, with summary of key issues, see *The Treaty Establishing a Constitution for Europe*, published by the British Management Data Foundation www.bmdf.co.uk.

26 Article 43 TEU.

27 Milne, *A Cost Too Far?*, 2004.

NB: For detailed bullet-point analyses of the above, supported by official figures and impeccable sources, see also the Briefing Notes and other material on www.globalbritain.org.

The Case for Staying In

Stephen Pollard

The debate over the direction of the EU has long been bedeviled by lies, half-truths and misleading statements. Many Eurofederalists who wish to see the EU turn into a 'superstate' to rival the US deny any such intention. Many Europhobes who wish to see Britain pull out describe themselves as Eurosceptics, lest their true views horrify their fellow countrymen and women. Caught in the crossfire between both sides' repeated assertions and distortions are an ever-more-bored and bewildered public.

Things do, at last, seem to be changing. The rise of UKIP in the 2004 Euro elections (albeit followed by a sudden crash back to earth) began to bring into the open the hidden agenda of some Eurosceptics, and the proposed new constitution has laid bare some of the aims of the Eurofanatics.

The operative words here are 'many' and 'some'. It should be a truism that not all Europhiles want to see the effective abolition of the UK as a self-governing, independent state, and that not all Eurosceptics want Britain to pull out of the EU. It should be a truism, but it does nonetheless need to be emphasised. Both positions are entirely honourable and deserve serious discussion. But they should not distract from the reality of political life which is that both extremes are supported only by small minorities of the population. The majority support continued membership of the EU but are, in the loose sense of the word, Eurosceptic. They want, to coin a phrase, to be 'in Europe but not run by Europe'.

As the following Mori poll shows, only 19 per cent of voters are 'strongly opposed' to UK membership:

Which of the following best describes your own
view of British membership of the European Union ?

(%)

- I strongly support British membership of the   16
  European Union

- I am generally in favour of British membership of the   34
  European Union, but could be persuaded against if I
  thought it would be bad for Britain

- I am generally opposed to British membership of the   22
  European Union, but could be persuaded in favour if I
  thought it would be good for Britain

- I strongly oppose British membership of the   19
  European Union

- Don't know   9

Source: *Mori*, 6 September 2004.

In responding to the argument that Britain would be better off out of the EU, one cannot escape a simple but pivotal fact. It comes down, in the end, to politics, and to a choice which is about far more than simple economics and figures. Those who wish to leave the EU do so not simply because, on a profit and loss account, they argue that we would be better off (although I would contend—and hope to prove—that they are wrong even on that basis) but because they do not agree with the very idea of the EU. That is a perfectly valid position which is not remotely 'Little Englander', as Eurofanatics would have it. (I worked for some years for Lord Shore of Stepney, one of the leaders of the 'No' campaign in the 1975 referendum. The notion that a man who carried a copy of the United Nations charter with him in his breast pocket, but who happened not to believe in the idea of the EU, was a Little Englander is simply risible.) But it is a position which needs to be stated baldly. Their agenda is not reform. Their complaints about the proposed constitution are, in a sense, irrelevant. They do not want to be a member of the EU, constitution or not. The choice which they advocate is not between competing visions of the EU. It is between being in or out. And if that is the choice which they seek to force, then I have no hesitation in saying 'in'.

It may be that we reach a position when the continued independence of the UK, and other nations which share our outlook, is incompatible with EU membership. That time is not, however, now. As an independent nation, we consent to reach joint decisions on certain areas of law with our fellow Member States. Contrary to the arguments of those who demand that we pull out now, we are not governed by the EU. We choose to reach decisions at an EU level. If, as a nation, we no longer choose to do that then we are free to leave. My contention is that such a choice is wrong.

Indeed, in pushing that choice, the 'outers' do immense harm to the cause of genuine Eurosceptics, who seek to build on what is now the opportunity of a generation to mould the EU in the direction which the British have been advocating for decades. The constitution, far from pushing us to the brink of withdrawal, offers the possibility of a wholesale rethink. The forthcoming referendum places the power to force change in the hands of the electorate, who will at last have the opportunity to say what they think, and to say it in a way which cannot be ignored. Europe's politicians would have no choice but to listen to—and take heed of—a 'No' vote, which would create an opportunity for genuine reform. Under EU law, every member state must approve the Constitution for it to come in to force. A 'No' vote will not mean the end of the EU—it will continue to run, as it does today—but it will create a perfect opportunity for reform by sending a sharp shock into the heart of the system.

Whatever the merits or otherwise of the proposed constitution, it is clear that something has to change. An EU of 25 members—or more, soon—is not the same as one of six (the number which signed the Treaty of Rome). Just as the institutional requirements are different, so too is the world in which the EU now operates. The Soviet Union and the Cold War are no more and the global economy is a reality, not a prediction. So it was right to re-set the foundations of the EU. The problem, however, is that the resetting took place along much the same lines as the old model, constructed by the archetypal Old Europe politician, Giscard D'Estaing, with no real input from lesser beings from New Europe. Now, however, we have the opportunity to change that.

Given the state of public opinion (polls record varying majorities against adoption of the constitution) and the predisposition of the press, it is hard to see how the 'yes' campaign might prevail. At a time when the possibility now exists of sending so severe a shock to the EU's system that change is unavoidable, it would be crazy, now of all times, to consider withdrawal. Not least, too, because the very membership of the EU has also changed forever the balance of forces between 'Old' and 'New' Europe. For years, the British pushed for enlargement, in part because it was a good thing in itself, but in part also because greater 'widening' was held to be a guarantor against greater 'deepening'. That widening is now with us. The force of history, and the balance of EU member states, is now on the side of those who want to see a more market-flexible, politically loose and sovereignty-respecting EU. Now is the time to use that advantage, not to turn into our shell and ignore it.

Living in Brussels for much of the year, there are few things more frustrating than being a British Eurosceptic. Not, one must hasten to add, because of the behaviour of other Europeans. The frustration begins and ends this side of the Eurostar terminal at Waterloo.

When I return home to London, I meet and talk with other Eurosceptics. Invariably the same thing happens: as they open their mouths, words come out that bear little relation to reality. As they speak, they talk about a caricature EU, stuck with a timewarp impression that has not been updated in the past 20 years. The EU they have in mind is, as Nick Ridley put it in 1990, 'a German racket designed to take over the whole of Europe', with the French 'behaving like poodles to the Germans'.

They seem wholly unaware that the EU is changing. It has enormous problems—such as the push towards a federal state inherent in the proposed new constitution—but the dynamics of the realpolitik which governs the EU are already in flux. Two critical developments mean that the Franco-German axis is no longer the dominant force. First, the statist, tax-devouring continental economic model is falling apart. Reality has ensured that even the inept German Chancellor, Gerhard Schröder, has started—however limply—to realise that reform is necessary.

Second, and more fundamentally, the accession of the ten new member states in 2004 has changed the mood music of the EU. The union has taken into its bosom countries which, far from wanting to form an alliance to take on the US, look to America as their saviour. The EU did nothing to free Poland, the Czech Republic, Estonia, Slovakia, Slovenia, Lithuania, Latvia and Hungary from the Soviet empire. They owe their freedom to the US. Indeed, many of their leading politicians were educated in the US and have been imbued with ideas of the free market and liberty.

When Donald Rumsfeld spoke in January 2003 of Old—and, by implication, New—Europe ('Germany has been a problem and France has been a problem. But you look at vast numbers of other countries in Europe, they're not with France and Germany... they're with the US. You're thinking of Europe as Germany and France. I don't. I think that's old Europe') he was spot on. These new countries' economies are light years away from those of Franco-German Old Europe. Estonia, for instance, introduced a stunningly successful flat tax rate of 26 per cent in 1994. In order to remain competitive with their neighbour, Lithuania and Latvia then introduced their own, which has prompted Estonia's plan to reduce its rate to 20 per cent within the next three years. Latvia is now reducing its corporate income tax rate to 19 per cent and Slovakia has brought in a flat 19 per cent rate for individuals and corporations.

In contrast, the Czech Republic has tried to ape Old Europe and has raised taxes and widened its welfare state. It is easy to see what will happen next: people and businesses will move to Slovakia and its economy will suffer.

The typical British Eurosceptic's response is to argue that this is all very well but irrelevant. The EU itself is the problem. And up to a point, yes. But the appointment of José Manuel Durão Barroso as President of the Commission is indicative of the new outlook. It is inconceivable that a man with his views could have been given such a job—by, remember, France and Germany—as little as five years ago. Barroso is certainly a convinced supporter of the EU. But he is also an Atlanticist, hosting—at considerable domestic political cost—talks between George W. Bush and Tony Blair in the Azores before the Iraq war, of which he was a supporter. He is a Portuguese version of Margaret Thatcher, ignoring uproar from the unions and less far-sighted colleagues to push through labour market and other free-market reforms. His allocation of portfolios provided further evidence of the new realpolitik within the EU— neither the German nor the French commissioner received a front rank responsibility, relegated to the relatively minor portfolios of Enterprise and Industry and Transport respectively.

It would be the ultimate in self-defeating irony if Britain turned its back on the EU at the very moment when the New Europe mindset is beginning to hold sway over Old Europe. It is, after all, the fruit of our success; it was British policy to widen the EU.

The real debate across the EU is much wider than Britain's exclusive focus on the constitution. It centres on whether the old sclerotic EU needs to change and introduce, albeit 20 years after Thatcher, market-friendly reforms. New Europe is winning, Old Europe losing, as Barroso's appointment shows. As the Polish economy grows, for example—in large part because of its access to the EU market—so too will its political influence.

Poland is not alone. Most of the new Member States, together with many of the existing ones, wanted to join the EU for two clear reasons: to stabilise and guarantee their political systems, and to have access to the largest market on the planet. Given the importance of both reasons, they have been prepared to put up with what has always been the other side of the coin—the *'acquis communautaire'*, and the drive led by Old Europe to an ever closer union. Their calculation was that political stability and economic prosperity far outweighed any possible loss of sovereignty.

British history, being very different, has meant that there has been no such consensus. We do not need to have our democracy guaranteed by an outside arrangement. Thus the argument has often been reduced solely to economic benefits.

But there has been too little recognition that the dominance of the Old Europe view has already begun to unravel. Eurosceptics pushed for a wider Europe to achieve a new balance of power within the EU. And guess what? They were right. The truth of the matter is that the very success of the existing, old, ever deeper model of the EU contained within its success—and the magnet effect it had on surrounding countries—the seeds of its own destruction, as those new countries applied for membership, were admitted, and then began to change the driving force within the EU.

Europhobes argue that this is fanciful—that there is no realistic prospect of a looser, less bureaucratic and centralised EU emerging anywhere other than in the heads of naïve Europhiles. But the evidence is already there of just such a possibility. Take the issue of returning existing EU competences to member states, rather than those extensions proposed in the new constitution. Even many Eurofanatics within Old Europe openly question the need for the Commission to be involved in so many areas of policy. And it is not just in Eastern and Central Europe where such debates are already widespread. In Scandinavia and the Netherlands one would be hard pressed to find a serious Europhile politician who does not accept the need for redrawing of the balance of competences. The political success of groups such as the June List in Sweden, which opposes the centralising thrust of the Old Europe, but remains in favour of continued Swedish membership, is typical. Such groups have an influence on the politics of their own native countries, but are also a classic example of the sum being greater than the individual parts, in promising a check on deepening and a new awareness of the need for flexibility. The single market is a typical example of how what should be a liberalising measure has been used to expand the EU's areas of influence, as fields which are not covered in the EU's governing treaties are 'smuggled in' as being relevant to the creation of the single market. There is, however, an alternative, favoured by economic liberals, and it is this view for which the New Europe states are already beginning to push.

Derek Scott, former economic adviser to Tony Blair, puts it thus:

> Economic liberals have a clear notion of what would constitute a single market in the EU. It would be in place when labour, goods, services and capital can flow as freely between countries as within any one of them. Policy is therefore directed at removing barriers that prevent this happening. People differ in their enthusiasm for this within Anglo-Saxon economies and getting to an approximation of this 'ideal' will take time, but in principle the destination and its framework are clear and requires very limited common standards let alone 'harmonisation' to make it work. However, there is another view of a single market reflected in the so-called European social model, or 'Rhenish capitalism'. This was successful for many years after the Second World War, but there were very particular and temporary features in the post-war years that haven't existed for some time and this model is less well suited to the modern world. [1]

This is the heart of the clash between competing visions of the EU. Is competition about a 'level playing field', in which EU standards are imposed across the board as a means of shackling those member states which seek to gain a competitive advantage through, for instance, labour market flexibility and tax policy? Or is it about allowing the market to do its job and allocate resources most efficiently? As Scott puts it:

> In a market economy, the fewer opportunities for competition and prices to allocate resources, the bigger the final distortion. In much of Europe this is reflected in lost output and jobs. When competition and markets are working properly there will be a tendency for some

convergence of labour standards, tax and a raft of other things. However, a prior imposition of a so-called level playing field actually prevents markets operating efficiently. There is a huge difference between a level playing field emerging as a result of competition working through properly functioning markets and being imposed in advance to reduce the implications of competition.[2]

The idea of pulling out at the very moment when the accession of new Member States has made possible, for the first time, the adoption of a more market-friendly environment is simply bizarre—not least because it plays straight into the hands of the government and those who want to see the constitution adopted. The government seeks to portray the referendum as being about 'in' or 'out'. It is not. It is about what type of EU we want. Do we want a flexible organisation in which states co-operate for their own mutual benefit, or do we want a centralised supra-national body which dictates terms and which we are powerless to resist?

By fighting on the government's terms, and urging that the issue really is 'in' or 'out', Europhobes guarantee that the reform case will be lost. Just as the polls show a large majority against the constitution, so too they show the same majority in favour of continued membership and against pulling out. If the 'No' campaign were to be taken over by those in favour of leaving, and who then urged that the referendum be treated as an 'in' or 'out' question, the public would, as all poll evidence suggests, vote to stay in, and thus to support the constitution, when if the argument over the constitution is treated on its merits—not about 'in' or 'out' but about the merits or otherwise of the constitution, the result would be a triumph for reformers. The withdrawal issue is thus political stupidity of the highest order, given the opportunity for a resettlement of the EU's foundations which would be presented by a 'No' vote.

There is, of course, no guarantee that the new alliances within the EU will indeed alter the direction taken. That is something for which we, and the other countries which think like Britain, will have to work. But there is, by definition, a guarantee of failure if Britain, to which New Europe invariably looks for solidity, were to pull out. The accession of Romania and Bulgaria in 2008/09 necessitates another treaty, come what may. We have the time to win.

The Case for Staying In

1   Scott, D., Speech to Vote No, 27 October 2004.

2   Scott, Speech to Vote No, 2004.